This Journal Belongs to:

_____

"If my friend ain't got no money And I say "take all mine, honey" "Taint nobody's bizness if I do, do', do do"

- Bessie Smith

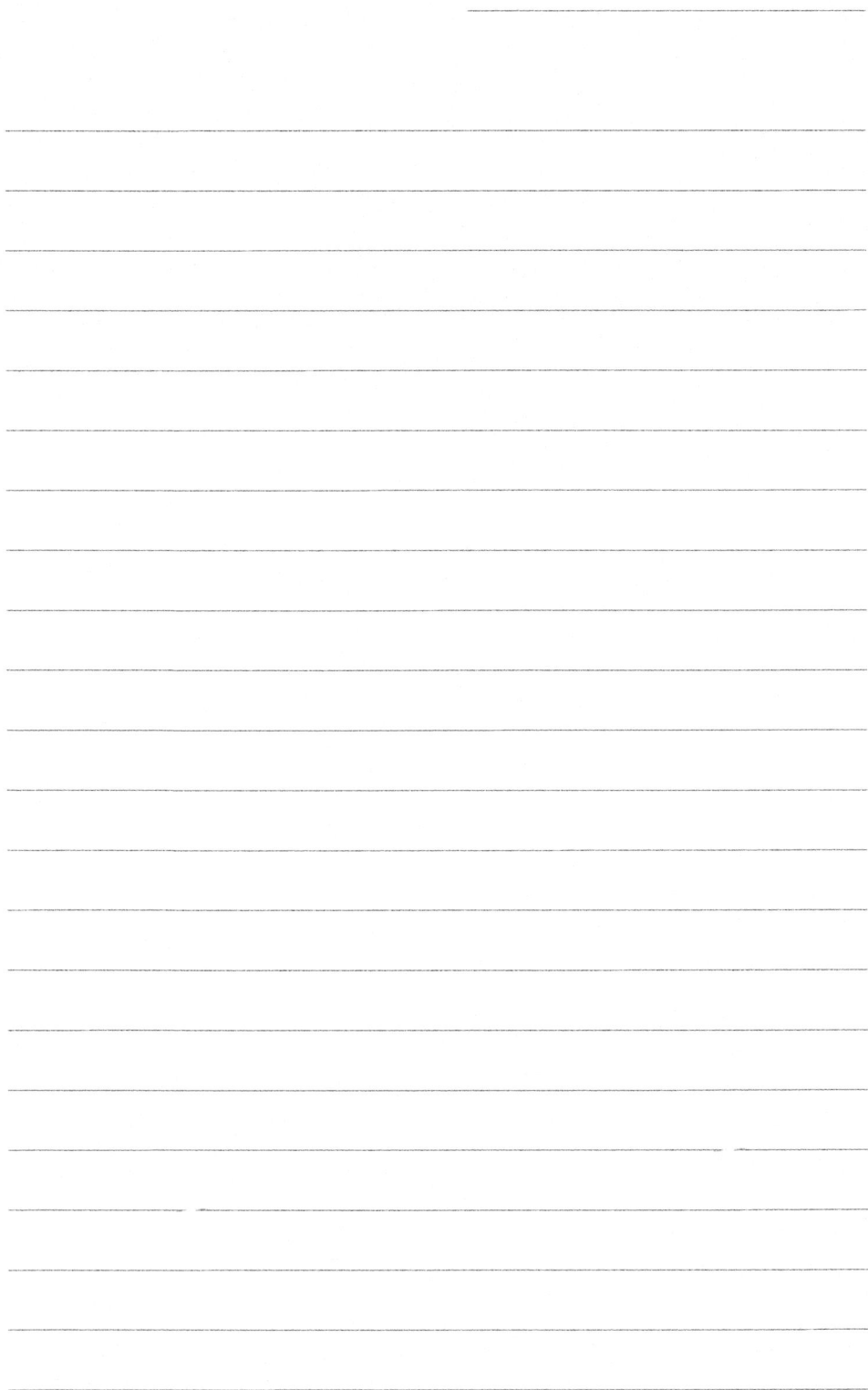

Made in the USA
Las Vegas, NV
24 December 2020